c

AF443563

Date Due

JUL 1 1980	JUL 10 2002	
JUN 2 3 1981	OCT 8 2003	
AUG 1 1 1981		
JUN 1 5 1982	MAR 2 0 2003	
7-6-82		
JUN 1 0 1986	JUL 0 2003	
MAR 1 0 1988		
SEP 2 8 1988		
JUL 2 4 1989		
DEC 1 3 1989		

DISCARD

Published by Creative Educational Society, Inc., 123 South Broad Street, Mankato, Minnesota 56001. Copyright © 1976 by Creative Educational Society, Inc. International copyrights reserved in all countries. No part of this book may be reproduced in any form without written permission from the publisher. Printed in the United States.
Library of Congress Cataloging in Publication Data
Braun, Thomas, 1944—
A. J. Foyt.
SUMMARY: A biography of the winner of more championship races than any other driver in the history of the United States Auto Club.
1. Foyt, A. J., 1935- —Juvenile literature. 2. Automobile racing—Juvenile literature.
[1. Foyt, A. J., 1935-   2. Automobile racing—Biography] I. Keely, John. II. Title.
GV1032.F66B72   796.7'2'0924 [B] [92]   76-12627   ISBN 0-87191-282-1

A. J. Foyt

By Thomas Braun

Illustrated by John Keely

Some people call him the "old man." At age 40 he has won more championship races than any other driver in the history of the United States Auto Club (USAC). Three times he's taken the checkered flag at the Indianapolis 500 race. Only three other drivers can match that accomplishment.

Sometimes he thinks and even talks about retirement, but his goal — the thing that drives him — is to become the only four-time winner of the Memorial Day race.

A victory at Indianapolis in 1975 would have made a perfect ending for the story of his brilliant career, but the time wasn't right. The racing world must not have been ready for the story to end. He didn't win the race. So, A. J. Foyt, the old man, just keeps on driving.

Conversations between real race fanatics are often filled with mysterious abbreviations ("The M-D blowers boosted the Offy's power up to 540"). It's not necessary, however, to be a fanatic to recognize the initials "A. J." and the number "500." People who have only a slight interest in auto racing know that the initials belong to only one driver and the number, although there are several other 500-mile races, refers to only one race.

The recent histories of both the Indianapolis 500 and A. J. Foyt are so closely tied together that it is difficult to talk about one "classic" without also talking about the other.

For one month each year a small world with sounds and smells and tensions all its own comes to life in central Indiana. Located at the western edge of Indianapolis, this temporary world called the Speedway occupies less than 450 acres. At its center is a 2½-mile paved oval track. On this track the best drivers in auto racing compete to win the sport's richest and most dramatic contest, the Indy 500.

As the end of May approaches, the Speedway undergoes an instant population explosion. The area is suddenly packed with drivers, mechanics, car-owners, track officials, and, of course, the largest and most diverse group of all, the race fans.

Like the drivers, some of these spectators are veterans and others are rookies. The veteran can talk easily about things like "four-cycle overhead camshafts" and "maximum piston displacement." He's read about the newest improvements in engines, tires, and suspensions. He probably has a hero, a driver whose career he

has followed closely.

The rookie fan may also come to the Speedway with expectations; but without first acquiring some fundamental information about the race, he may leave the track with only vague impressions of loud noise and blurred motion.

Although the 500 receives the greatest amount of publicity, the race itself is only one event in a year-long series of 12 races sanctioned by USAC. The entire series is usually referred to as the "Championship Trail." Drivers not only compete for prize money but also accumulate points. At the end of each season, the driver with the most points becomes the National Driving Champion.

In addition to scheduling races and naming a champion, USAC sets up rigid specifications for its cars. The size of the engine, the length and width of the body, and the over-all weight of the racing machine are only a few of the items covered by a long list of USAC

restrictions.

The championship car or "Indy car" as it is sometimes called, has a single seat, an open cockpit, and "open wheels" (its tires are not enclosed by fenders). Its engine, located in the rear, is capable of developing as much as 900 horsepower. Most of the engines used today are manufactured by Ford or Offenhauser. All of the engines are "turbocharged;" that is, the air-fuel mixture is pumped directly into the engine instead of being drawn in by natural air pressure.

The Indy cars no longer run on gasoline. They now use an expensive blend of "methanol" and "nitromethane." Most cars travel less than two miles on a gallon of this fuel.

In order to minimize air resistance, the wedge-shaped body of the car is slung low between the four giant tires. Because the car reaches speeds close to 200 mph, the body must be designed to prevent the machine from losing contact with the track and actually flying.

Each driver is required to wear a uniform made of flame-resistant fabric. The lower half of his face is covered by a fire-proof mask; and his head is protected by a strong, lightweight helmet. The deafening scream of the engine makes earplugs necessary.

Since the height of the car is only 32 inches, the driver must recline rather than sit in his narrow compartment. Often traveling 250 feet per second, his body

rides less than four inches above the asphalt.

During the three-hour contest, the driver blasts through 200 counterclockwise laps. Working in temperatures that can top 145 degrees, he must negotiate a total of 800 left-hand turns and, all the while, avoid hitting the 32 other cars and the concrete retaining wall around the oval.

Although there are always favored cars and favored drivers, nothing is ever certain during a race. The machines are so complicated and the track conditions so varied that plans and predictions are impossible to make. Some drivers get lucky, survive the ordeal, and pocket hundreds of thousands of dollars. Others misjudge a turn, smash into another competitor, and don't survive at all.

The only certain advice about driving the 500 came from the two-time winner, Bill Vukovich. "Just remember one thing," he said. "Always turn left." Vukovich died in a crash at Indy in 1955.

Racing's most famous survivor, A. J. Foyt, started down the Championship Trail in 1975, intent on winning the 500. He had not won at Indianapolis since 1967 and, following that last win, had struggled through a long dry spell. Between 1969 and 1974 he had won a slim total of six races on the championship circuit. In 1970 and again in the 1972 season he had been shut out completely.

Foyt hates to lose. "Winning — that's what it's all about," he has said. "There's nothing on earth like it. It makes me sick any time I lose."

Tired of losing, tired of his own special sickness, A. J. opened the new 1975 season looking and driving like a young champion. In March he won a 100-mile qualifying race at Ontario, California. He came back one week later and, after leading 186 laps of the 200-lap race, won the California 500. Then in the first week of April he drove to another championship victory in New Jersey's Trenton 200.

With Indianapolis only one month off, Foyt's

number of championship wins during his entire career had reached 50. His closest competitor was Mario Andretti with 32. A. J.'s comeback was accelerating, gathering speed. Once again race fans and sportswriters looked ahead to the possibility of Foyt's winning his fourth 500.

By mid-April all entry forms for the Indy 500 must be filed with the track officials. Near the end of the month drivers and crews begin to arrive at the Speedway, towing their closely guarded machines. Throughout the preceding months, designers and mechanics have worked full-time preparing their cars for the big test.

Soon after their arrival, drivers undergo thorough physical examinations. Then they get ready for three long weeks of practice laps and qualification trials.

Usually between 70 and 90 drivers file entry forms. In 1975, however, because of general economic problems and the difficulty of attracting sponsorships, the field was limited to 56 cars. Whatever the number of entries, there are only 33 starting positions for the race.

The 33 starters begin the race positioned in 11 rows of three cars. Starting positions are determined during two weekends of qualifying runs. The best place to start the race is at the head of the pack on the inside of the first row. Always filled on the first day of qualifying, this spot is called the "pole position" and is almost as hotly contested as the race itself.

A. J. Foyt arrived at the Speedway with two bright-red Gilmore Coyotes (Indy cars are named for the sponsor, Gilmore, and for the make of the chassis, Coyote). He had driven his number 10 Coyote in early-season competition. The other Coyote, number 14, was a newer car with a much narrower body.

On Saturday, two weeks before the actual race, a huge qualifying-day crowd flooded the grandstands. The size of the crowd was estimated at over 200,000. By

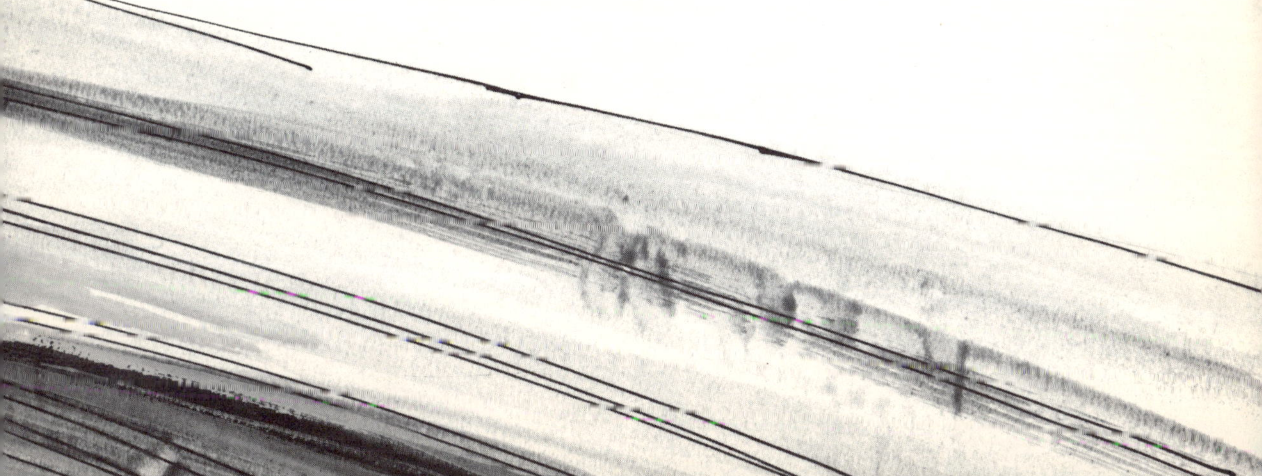

mid-day the sun had climbed high over the hot track. Foyt appeared in his narrow Coyote, and the spectators cheered. Clearly he was the sentimental favorite.

A. J. pushed hard on the first lap but was clocked at only 189.195 mph. That was the fastest speed of the morning, but A. J. knew that drivers behind him in the qualifying order could run much faster. Instead of finishing the four-lap qualifying trial, he returned to his pit area and decided to postpone his attempt until later in the day.

While Foyt's crew hovered over the Coyote, the average speeds gradually increased. Tom Sneva, a former junior high school principal, raised the mark to 190.094 mph. Bobby Unser climbed over 191 mph, and Gordon Johncock topped Unser with a 191.652 average.

A. J. waited. He knew the first round wouldn't close until 6 p.m. He would hold off until the track had a

GOOD/YEAR

chance to cool. The fans waited. Even the late afternoon sun seemed to wait from behind the west grandstand.

Finally the familiar red wedge appeared. A. J. slipped through a few practice laps then raised his hand to signal that he was ready to take a run against the clock.

For both the driver and the crowd, the wait was worth it. On his first lap he hit 195.313 mph. After three more laps his average was posted: 193.976 — more than two miles faster than the previous leader. The crowd roared. A. J. had clinched the pole position for the 1975 Indy 500.

Having qualified on the first day, A. J. had two weeks to calculate his race strategy and make further adjustments on his car. Race drivers have a habit of looking ahead. It's unlikely that A. J.'s busy pre-race schedule allowed him any time for looking back.

Anthony Joseph Foyt, Jr. started to learn about cars and how to drive them when he was very young. His first teacher was his father who owned a garage in Houston, Texas. Tony Sr. had driven both midget cars and stock cars on local dirt tracks. When A. J. was only four years old, Tony built a miniature red racing car for his son. Since that first experience behind a steering wheel, A. J. has devoted his life to building and driving the fastest cars in auto racing.

In high school A. J. made a decision which surprised no one. His ambition and confidence were so

clear that, at age 17, he dropped out of school and entered professional racing.

He combined part-time work at his father's garage with as many races as he could enter. He drove every kind of vehicle on every kind of track. He raced jalopies, stock cars, and even motorcycles. Competition on the small-town tracks in the Southwest was always fast and brutal; but always A. J. seemed faster, tougher, and more skillful.

He soon moved into midget racing and put together such an impressive record in that category that several owners of championship cars expressed an inter-

est in hiring him. Foyt drove his first USAC championship race in 1957.

The next logical step up for the young driver was
Indianapolis. Each May for three years Foyt scraped
together enough money to buy himself a seat in the

grandstand at the Speedway. He studied the track, carefully checking each turn for its own unique characteristics. He studied the cars, listened to the mechanics, and, whenever possible, talked to the drivers.

At the end of the 1957 Indy 500, A. J. left the Speedway as a spectator for the last time. The following year he was offered his first chance to drive a big car in the biggest of all races.

When A. J. Foyt, the driver, first arrived at the Speedway in 1958, he may have looked young; but he was certainly not inexperienced. No sponsor is ever willing to gamble his huge investment on a driver who has not already shown strength, quick reflexes, and intelligence.

As a further check on a driver's readiness, a first-time contestant at Indy must pass a driving test. The rookie test is a series of laps which must be driven at a predetermined speed. USAC officials and a group of veteran drivers carefully observe the rookie's performance. If his speed varies too much or if his behavior is erratic in any way, the driver is automatically eliminated.

A. J. had no problem passing the rookie test. His performance on qualifying day was even better. He won a starting position on the outside of the fourth row ahead of 21 other drivers.

On the first lap of the race, two cars, both fighting for the lead, missed the third turn and slammed into the wall. Both cars were destroyed. One driver was hurt, the other was uninjured; but the collision wasn't finished.

Coming up on the wreckage, a third driver hit his brakes too hard. A fourth car smashed into the third one. More cars — a total of 14 — added more torn metal, tires, and smoke to the mess. When the crunching stopped and the air cleared, Pat O'Connor, a young driver, was dead.

Somehow Foyt had avoided the wreck and had managed to take sixteenth place in his first race at Indy. Considering the day's massacre in Turn Three, A. J. had done well.

A. J. continued to race smaller cars on smaller dirt tracks across the country, and he continued to string together a long series of wins. Having smelled and tasted the excitement at Indianapolis, however, all of the other contests seemed insignificant.

He returned to the 500 in 1959 and placed tenth. The next year his clutch gave out after 90 laps, and he was unable to finish. That same year, Foyt won four of the other 11 races on the Championship Trail. At the end of the 1960 season he had the highest point total and had won his first USAC National Driving Championship.

On Memorial Day, 1961, the Speedway celebrated its fiftieth anniversary. Before the day ended, A. J. had his own reason for celebrating.

Back for his fourth year, he started the race on the inside of the third row. Soon after the start, a contest developed between A. J. and Eddie Sachs, a veteran who had never won the 500. All afternoon they traded the lead back and forth, always staying close together. By lap 180, Foyt led Sachs by three seconds. Then on lap 185, A. J.'s crew ordered him to stop for re-fueling. The stop was necessary but costly. Sachs shot a full 25 seconds ahead. Back in the race, A. J. kept pressing the leader. Time was running out. It looked hopeless.

But Indy has a way of evening things out at the last minute. With only three laps to go, Sachs noticed that his right rear tire was worn dangerously thin and would never hold together through the remaining laps. He pitted, picked up a new tire, and tore back onto the track; but it was too late. The young challenger from Texas was too far ahead. A. J. took the checkered flag. He had won his first 500.

A. J.'s best year in racing will probably be the

year he wins his fourth 500. Until then, 1967 stands as
the highpoint of his career.

He had taken his second win at Indianapolis in
1965. Then during the next two years his luck seemed to
change. He demolished one car at Indy and barely
survived a fiery crash during the Riverside 500 stock car
race. In 1966 he failed to win a single championship race.

Next to Foyt's bad fortune, the most popular topic of conversation at Indianapolis in 1967 was a new kind of car. During the 1960s, the Speedway fans had watched the introduction and slow acceptance of the lighter, faster, rear-engine car. Just when the dust from the rear-engine revolution had finally settled, Andy Granatelli came along and tried to start another revolution. At the 1967 race, Granatelli introduced the STP Turbocar.

The new machine was powered by a gas-turbine engine much like the one used in small planes and boats. A big advantage of the new engine was that it had fewer moving parts than the standard piston engine. That meant fewer parts to break down during the long race. The most distinctive feature and the thing that bothered the skeptics the most was the near-silence of the new car.

Everyone was willing to accept changes and improvements in Indy cars, but a car without ear-splitting noise could not be trusted.

Parnelli Jones moved the new car through a few practice laps, and momentarily the critics were quieter than the car. It had blazing, blinding speed not only down the straightaways but also in the turns.

A. J. Foyt was among the drivers who complained the loudest about the Turbocar. "I've always thought the Indianapolis Speedway is a proving ground for cars, not airplanes," he said.

When the race started, Jones flew out ahead of the field and stayed there. Driving his first Coyote which he had built himself in Texas, A. J. held on to second place. Unless the Turbocar fell apart, it was clear that A. J. had no chance of catching and passing Jones.

On lap 197 history repeated itself. With three laps left in the 1961 race, Eddie Sachs had been forced to stop for a new tire, and A. J. had won. In 1967, with those same three laps remaining, the Turbocar burned out a $6 bearing in its gearbox and quietly dropped out of the contest. As he had six years earlier, A. J. survived and won.

Winning his third 500 should have been enough for one year, but A. J. has never been easily satisfied. Two weeks after beating the Turbocar, Foyt went to France to compete in the Le Mans Endurance Race.

Le Mans is a 24-hour race driven on an irregular, 8.3-mile road course. Two drivers alternate shifts at the wheel of their car. Obviously this kind of race is very different from oval-track competition. Most people thought that A. J. would not be able to adjust to the different track conditions and driving techniques of Le Mans.

They were wrong. The team of Dan Gurney and A. J. Foyt won the race and in the process set a new speed record. Even more important, A. J. demonstrated his versatility as a driver. Within two weeks he had won the two most important races in the world, and that double win made 1967 a very good year.

The Indianapolis 500 is a spectacular annual

ritual. From year to year a few things change, but race fans keep going back because they know that the important things — speed, excitement, and danger — will always be there.

On the night before the 1975 race, thousands of spectators have already gathered at the Speedway. They are waiting for the gates to open at 4 a.m. They stop their various celebrations long enough to watch a total eclipse of the moon.

The shadow over the moon moves on. The silence over the crowd doesn't last long. Things get back to normal quickly.

It's still dark when the gates finally open. The spectators swarm over the infield looking for places to set down their heavy coolers and set up their folding chairs. Some people can afford the high ticket prices for grandstand seats. They won't arrive until after sunrise. Others pay as much as $20,000 per year to lease luxury suites overlooking Turn Two. They won't arrive until just before the race starts.

At 7:30 a.m. the gate to Gasoline Alley opens. Each car is pushed out of its garage and towed to its designated pit area.

Around 8:30 a.m. a parade starts down the main straightaway. The temperature is already close to 80 degrees. It's hot and humid.

At 9 a.m. each crew maneuvers its car into starting position. When the cars are in place, fireworks explode, signaling that the start is near. The explosion is also a kind of alarm clock for the people who have had too much beer and fried chicken and have fallen asleep. To make sure that everyone's awake, a band plays "Back Home Again in Indiana."

Each driver is introduced. Because he won the pole position two weeks earlier, A. J. Foyt is introduced first. The fans roar. He lifts his hand briefly, acknowledging their support.

The other 32 drivers are introduced. The announcer gives his familiar command: "Gentlemen, start your engines!" The crews attach portable starters to the cars. Within seconds howling engines echo through the Speedway. To some it sounds like beautiful music. A. J.

tightens his shoulder harness inside his own howling
Coyote.

The pace car slowly advances. The anxious field
of racers follows close behind. After two laps the pace car
disappears into the infield. The drivers get the green
flag, and the race is on.

A. J. is after his fourth.

The start of the race is always a dangerous time.
Drivers try to improve their positions in a field that is
always bunched closely together. This start is smooth.

Gordon Johncock jumps ahead of Foyt and
Bobby Unser. On the ninth lap A. J. makes a move and
passes Johncock. Two laps later Johncock drops out

with mechanical problems, an early casualty.

Another big name runs into trouble. Mario Andretti leans too far out in the third turn, smacks the wall, and drops out of the contest. Wally Dallenbach in third place has no trouble passing Johnny Rutherford. On lap 60 Dallenbach whips past A. J.'s Coyote and soon opens up a 20 second lead.

Tom Sneva's rear wheel slides into another car. Sneva's car flips up, breaks apart as it hits the wall, and explodes. Somehow Sneva is rescued. His hands and face are badly burned.

Foyt drives over some of the wreckage and pulls in to have his tires checked. By the time he gets back on the track, he's slipped to fourth place.

Dallnebach, the leader, burns out a piston. He's finished.

Other shadows begin to move over the Speedway. Not an eclipse, this time it's rain.

Bobby Unser leads. Foyt is third. A. J. has come from behind at the last minute several times before, but it doesn't happen this time. The rain increases. The cars can barely stay on the flooded track. The red flag comes out to stop the race, and Unser is declared the winner.

A young driver once said, "There are so many factors, so much luck involved in winning at Indy that to do it once is almost a miracle."

A. J. Foyt has done it three times, and he's still out there trying to make it four.

GOODYEAR

Football
Johnny Unitas
Bob Griese
Vince Lombardi
Joe Namath
O. J. Simpson
Fran Tarkenton
Roger Staubach
Alan Page
Larry Csonka
Don Shula
Franco Harris
Terry Bradshaw
Chuck Foreman
Ken Stabler

Baseball
Frank Robinson
Tom Seaver
Jackie Robinson
Johnny Bench
Hank Aaron
Roberto Clemente
Mickey Mantle
Rod Carew
Fred Lynn
Pete Rose

Basketball
Walt Frazier
Kareem Abdul Jabbar
Wilt Chamberlain
Jerry West
Bill Russell
Bill Walton
Bob McAdoo
Julius Erving
John Havlicek
Rick Barry
George McGinnis
Dave Cowens
Pete Maravich

superstars! superstars! superstars!

CREATIVE EDUCATION SPORTS SUPERSTARS

Golf
Lee Trevino
Jack Nicklaus
Arnold Palmer
Johnny Miller
Kathy Whitworth
Laura Baugh

Tennis
Jimmy Connors
Chris Evert
Pancho Gonzales
Evonne Goolagong
Arthur Ashe
Billie Jean King
Stan Smith

Miscellaneous
Mark Spitz
Muhammad Ali
Secretariat
Olga Korbut
Evel Knievel
Jean Claude Killy
Janet Lynn
Peggy Fleming
Pelé
Rosi Mittermaier
Sheila Young
Dorothy Hamill
Nadia Comaneci

Hockey
Phil and Tony Esposito
Gordie Howe
Bobby Hull
Bobby Orr

Racing
Peter Revson
Jackie Stewart
A.J. Foyt
Richard Petty